FRANCIS FRITH'S

DORCHESTER PHOTOGRAPHIC MEMORIES

THE FRANCIS FRITH COLLECTION

www.francisfrith.com

Photographic Memories

Francis Frith's
Around Dorchester

Christine McGee

First published in the United Kingdom in 2001 by
The Francis Frith Collection

Paperback Edition 2001
ISBN 1-85937-307-0

British Library Cataloguing in Publication Data

Francis Frith's Around Dorchester
Christine McGee

The Francis Frith Collection
Frith's Barn, Teffont,
Salisbury, Wiltshire SP3 5QP
Tel: +44 (0) 1722 716 376
Email: info@francisfrith.co.uk
www.francisfrith.com

Printed and bound in Great Britain

Front Cover: **Dorchester, Cornhill 1922** 72741t

The colour-tinting is for illustrative purposes only, and is not intended to be historically accurate

Contents

Francis Frith: *Victorian Pioneer*

FRANCIS FRITH, Victorian founder of the world-famous photographic archive, was a complex and multi-talented man. A devout Quaker and a highly successful Victorian businessman, he was both philosophic by nature and pioneering in outlook.

By 1855 Francis Frith had already established a wholesale grocery business in Liverpool, and sold it for the astonishing sum of £200,000, which is the equivalent today of over £15,000,000. Now a multi-millionaire, he was able to indulge his passion for travel. As a child he had pored over travel books written by early explorers, and his fancy and imagination had been stirred by family holidays to the sublime mountain regions of Wales and Scotland. 'What a land of spirit-stirring and enriching scenes and places!' he had written. He was to return to these scenes of grandeur in later years to 'recapture the thousands of vivid and tender memories', but with a different purpose. Now in his thirties, and captivated by the new science of photography, Frith set out on a series of pioneering journeys to the Nile regions that occupied him from 1856 until 1860.

Intrigue and Adventure

He took with him on his travels a specially-designed wicker carriage that acted as both dark-room and sleeping chamber. These far-flung journeys were packed with intrigue and adventure. In his life story, written when he was sixty-three, Frith tells of being held captive by bandits, and of fighting 'an awful midnight battle to the very point of surrender with a deadly pack of hungry, wild dogs'. Sporting flowing Arab costume, Frith arrived at Akaba by camel seventy years before Lawrence, where he encountered 'desert princes and rival sheikhs, blazing with jewel-hilted swords'.

During these extraordinary adventures he was assiduously exploring the desert regions bordering the Nile and patiently recording the antiquities and peoples with his camera. He was the first photographer to venture beyond the sixth cataract. Africa was still the mysterious 'Dark Continent', and Stanley and Livingstone's historic meeting was a decade into the future. The conditions for picture taking confound belief. He laboured for hours in his wicker dark-room in the sweltering heat of the desert, while the volatile chemicals fizzed dangerously in their trays. Often he was forced to work in remote tombs and caves where conditions were cooler. Back in London he exhibited his photographs and was 'rapturously cheered' by members of the Royal Society. His reputation as a photographer was made overnight. An eminent modern historian has likened their impact on the population of the time to that on our own generation of the first photographs taken on the surface of the moon.

Venture of a Life-Time

Characteristically, Frith quickly spotted the opportunity to create a new business as a specialist publisher of photographs. He lived in an era of immense and sometimes violent change. For the poor in the early part of Victoria's reign work was a drudge and the hours long, and people had precious little free time to enjoy themselves. Most had no transport other than a cart or gig at their disposal, and had not travelled far beyond the boundaries of their own town or village. However,

by the 1870s, the railways had threaded their way across the country, and Bank Holidays and half-day Saturdays had been made obligatory by Act of Parliament. All of a sudden the ordinary working man and his family were able to enjoy days out and see a little more of the world.

With characteristic business acumen, Francis Frith foresaw that these new tourists would enjoy having souvenirs to commemorate their days out. In 1860 he married Mary Ann Rosling and set out with the intention of photographing every city, town and village in Britain. For the next thirty years he travelled the country by train and by pony and trap, producing fine photographs of seaside resorts and beauty spots that were keenly bought by millions of Victorians. These prints were painstakingly pasted into family albums and pored over during the dark nights of winter, rekindling precious memories of summer excursions.

The Rise of Frith & Co

Frith's studio was soon supplying retail shops all over the country. To meet the demand he gathered about him a small team of photographers, and published the work of independent artist-photographers of the calibre of Roger Fenton and Francis Bedford. In order to gain some understanding of the scale of Frith's business one only has to look at the catalogue issued by Frith & Co in 1886: it runs to some 670 pages, listing not only many thousands of views of the British Isles but also many photographs of most European countries, and China, Japan, the USA and Canada – note the sample page shown above from the hand-written *Frith & Co* ledgers detailing pictures taken. By 1890 Frith had created the greatest specialist photographic publishing company in the

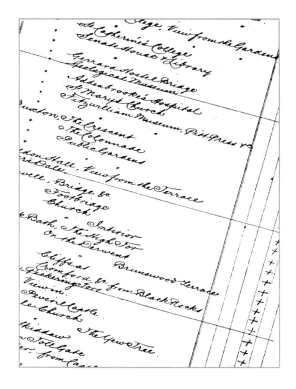

Frith's death, a new card measuring 5.5 x 3.5 inches became the standard format, but it was not until 1902 that the divided back came into being, with address and message on one face and a full-size illustration on the other. *Frith & Co* were in the vanguard of postcard development, and Frith's sons Eustace and Cyril continued their father's monumental task, expanding the number of views offered to the public and recording more and more places in Britain, as the coasts and countryside were opened up to mass travel.

Francis Frith died in 1898 at his villa in Cannes, his great project still growing. The archive he created continued in business for another seventy years. By 1970 it contained over a third of a million pictures of 7,000 cities, towns and villages. The massive photographic record Frith has left to us stands as a living monument to a special and very remarkable man.

world, with over 2,000 outlets – more than the combined number that Boots and W H Smith have today! The picture on the right shows the *Frith & Co* display board at Ingleton in the Yorkshire Dales. Beautifully constructed with mahogany frame and gilt inserts, it could display up to a dozen local scenes.

Postcard Bonanza

The ever-popular holiday postcard we know today took many years to develop. In 1870 the Post Office issued the first plain cards, with a pre-printed stamp on one face. In 1894 they allowed other publishers' cards to be sent through the mail with an attached adhesive halfpenny stamp. Demand grew rapidly, and in 1895 a new size of postcard was permitted called the court card, but there was little room for illustration. In 1899, a year after

Frith's Archive: *A Unique Legacy*

FRANCIS FRITH'S legacy to us today is of immense significance and value, for the magnificent archive of evocative photographs he created provides a unique record of change in 7,000 cities, towns and villages throughout Britain over a century and more. Frith and his fellow studio photographers revisited locations many times down the years to update their views, compiling for us an enthralling and colourful pageant of British life and character.

We tend to think of Frith's sepia views of Britain as nostalgic, for most of us use them to conjure up memories of places in our own lives with which we have family associations. It often makes us forget that to Francis Frith they were records of daily life as it was actually being lived in the cities, towns and villages of his day. The Victorian age was one of great and often bewildering change for ordinary people, and though the pictures evoke an impression of slower times, life was as busy and hectic as it is today.

We are fortunate that Frith was a photographer of the people, dedicated to recording the minutiae of everyday life. For it is this sheer wealth of visual data, the painstaking chronicle of changes in dress, transport, street layouts, buildings, housing, engineering and landscape that captivates us so much today. His remarkable images offer us a powerful link with the past and with the lives of our ancestors.

Today's Technology

Computers have now made it possible for Frith's many thousands of images to be accessed almost instantly. In the Frith archive today, each photograph is carefully 'digitised' then stored on a CD Rom. Frith archivists can locate a single photograph amongst thousands within seconds. Views can be catalogued and sorted under a variety of categories of place and content to the immediate benefit of researchers.

Inexpensive reference prints can be created for them at the touch of a mouse button, and a wide range of books and other printed materials assembled and published for a wider, more general readership - in the next twelve months over a hundred Frith local history titles will be published! The day-to-day workings of the archive are very different from how they were in Francis Frith's time: imagine the herculean task of sorting through eleven tons of glass negatives as Frith had to do to locate a particular sequence of pictures! Yet the

See Frith at www.francisfrith.com

archive still prides itself on maintaining the same high standards of excellence laid down by Francis Frith, including the painstaking cataloguing and indexing of every view.

It is curious to reflect on how the internet now allows researchers in America and elsewhere greater instant access to the archive than Frith himself ever enjoyed. Many thousands of individual views can be called up on screen within seconds on one of the Frith internet sites, enabling people living continents away to revisit the streets of their ancestral home town, or view places in Britain where they have enjoyed holidays. Many overseas researchers welcome the chance to view special theme selections, such as transport, sports, costume and ancient monuments.

We are certain that Francis Frith would have heartily approved of these modern developments in imaging techniques, for he himself was always working at the very limits of Victorian photographic technology.

The Value of the Archive Today

Because of the benefits brought by the computer, Frith's images are increasingly studied by social historians, by researchers into genealogy and ancestory, by architects, town planners, and by teachers and schoolchildren involved in local history projects.

In addition, the archive offers every one of us an opportunity to examine the places where we and our families have lived and worked down the years. Highly successful in Frith's own era, the archive is now, a century and more on, entering a new phase of popularity.

The Past in Tune with the Future

Historians consider the Francis Frith Collection to be of prime national importance. It is the only archive of its kind remaining in private ownership and has been valued at a million pounds. However, this figure is now rapidly increasing as digital technology enables more and more people around the world to enjoy its benefits.

Francis Frith's archive is now housed in an historic timber barn in the beautiful village of Teffont in Wiltshire. Its founder would not recognize the archive office as it is today. In place of the many thousands of dusty boxes containing glass plate negatives and an all-pervading odour of photographic chemicals, there are now ranks of computer screens. He would be amazed to watch his images travelling round the world at unimaginable speeds through network and internet lines.

The archive's future is both bright and exciting. Francis Frith, with his unshakeable belief in making photographs available to the greatest number of people, would undoubtedly approve of what is being done today with his lifetime's work. His photographs, depicting our shared past, are now bringing pleasure and enlightenment to millions around the world a century and more after his death.

Around Dorchester - *An Introduction*

AROUND 70-80AD THE GOVERNOR of Britannia, Agricola, decided that the province was now secure, and ordered towns to be built. In Dorset the Romans built Durnovaria, which has since become known as Dorchester.

The Romans had arrived in about 44AD, and subjugated the native tribe, the Durotriges. These Iron Age people lived in a huge hillfort, known today as Maiden Castle. Led by Vespasian, the Legion II Augusta was an efficient fighting machine, typical of the Roman army, and the Romans soon overcame any resistance that the Durotriges were able to muster. For many years following this battle most of the local people seem to have remained close to Maiden Castle.

To the Romans, living in towns was the way to civilisation. For the important buildings - the temple, the baths and the basilica, which was the office of local government - money was provided from Rome; these prestigious buildings would have left the native people in no doubt as to who was in charge. The Durotriges would have built their own houses and workshops initially of wood, but later of stone or flint and brick. The remains of one such site was discovered in Colliton Park in the 1930s, and is now on public display. Durnovaria thrived and became the civitas, or administrative centre, of the region. The town stood at the crossroads of an important road from Weymouth, which probably went as far as Bristol, and the Via Iceniana, which linked Exeter with London.

Early in the 2nd century, the occupants of Durnovaria began fortifying the town, building a surrounding wall and three great ditches.

The town remained within the line of this wall until the middle of the 19th century, when the railway was constructed. Little remains of the walls as they were, because in the 18th century the remnants were levelled and laid out as attractive tree-lined walks. A short length of the rubble core of the original Roman wall can be seen close to the Top o'Town. Maumbury Rings, the Roman amphitheatre to the south of the town, has a previous history as one of the many Neolithic henge monuments that have been found in the area.

Durnovaria declined in the late Roman period, particularly after the army was finally withdrawn in 410. Trade with the continent ceased, money no longer came from Rome, and life gradually became more difficult for the residents. The Anglo-Saxons, who were a warring tribe, were invading Britain. They drove many of the Romano-British west into Wales. Those who remained had to learn to live alongside a new occupying force. The Anglo-Saxons were not as civilised as the Romans. They had little use for the temples, baths and other signs of Roman sophistication, and they were probably the first to begin the robbing of Roman buildings for stone or other building materials. There is evidence of vandalism in the house in Colliton Park : most of the pillars from the veranda were deposited in the well, and a fire was made on the mosaic floor of one of the main rooms of the house.

In time, the Saxons became more educated; and slowly the people became settled into a rural community, though it was not always peaceful. The town was made a burgh: it would have held a market, and would continue to be a centre of administration for the surrounding area.

When the Viking raids began in 789, the king's reeve, or representative, travelled from Dorchester to Portland hoping to find traders, and was murdered for his pains. The presence of a reeve in Dorchester shows how important the town was. It is also said that King Alfred held councils in the town in 847 and 864 when he was planning how to overcome the Danes.

A wooden castle was built on a grassy knoll above the river at some time during the late Saxon or early Norman period, but it was destroyed in the 14th century, and the prison now stands in its place. Following the Norman invasion, Dorchester remained a small market town with administrative duties. During the time of King Edward the Confessor, in 1066, there were 172 houses in Dorchester. However, by 1088, according to the Domesday Book, only 88 remained. The destruction of one hundred houses seems to have been the work of King William's sheriff, Hugh fitz Gripp; the difference in the numbers shows that some of the houses had been rebuilt.

When Henry II, who reigned from 1154 to 1189,

introduced circuit Judges to hold the quarterly assize, he declared that the Dorset assizes should be held in Dorchester.

There has been a market here probably since Roman times, but certainly since the Saxon era. The continuity of this market has been the main support of the town's economy until the late 20th century. Dorchester is still dependent upon the rural economy.

A ship from Genoa anchored at Melcome Regis in 1348, and carried the Black Death to England; Dorchester was badly affected, and the population was more than halved. The disease spread rapidly, not only through Dorset but to the whole country.

In the 14th and 15th centuries the religious orders became strong and powerful, holding much of the land and collecting their tithes, or tenths, of their tenants' produce. Great tithe barns were built for storing their crops; at Abbotsbury and Cerne Abbas they still stand today, although the abbey buildings are all in ruins. The monasteries also kept large flocks of sheep on the surrounding chalk downlands.

The population recovered slowly during the 15th and 16th centuries. Mills were built along the river, including one at the foot of Friary Hill, and a flourmill and a sawmill were operating here in the 19th century. It is still described as Friary Mill, and it must have belonged to the 11th-century friary that stood where Orchard Street and Frome Terrace now stand. Like all the great abbeys, the friary was dissolved by Henry VIII at the Reformation.

In 1539 Henry VIII issued a charter which fully incorporated the borough and made Dorchester the shire town of Dorset. Later, Elizabeth I confirmed this.

In the 17th century there were several dreadful fires. In August 1613 a tallow chandler named Baker allowed his fire to get out of control. He had previously been warned by the constable, and this time the fire destroyed a great many of the timber-framed houses, which had thatched roofs. Soon afterwards, the corporation of the town decreed that no houses within the town walls could be built with thatched roofs.

From 1608 until 1648, the Rev John White was rector of Dorchester. He was a moderate Puritan, and he tried to keep his flock on the road to salvation. However, according to court records, there were plenty of people described as dissenters; these were not only Catholics, but also people who drank and danced on the Sabbath. There was much unrest in the countryside, and in 1630 there was a famine. Many of the agricultural labourers and their families sought refuge in the town. In order to assist them, John White, together with other local worthies, set up the Massachusetts Bay Company, and funded emigration to the New World. There were many difficulties, but the settlements survived: indeed,

today, there is a suburb of Boston, Massachusetts named Dorchester. The Civil War made further divisions between Dorchester and the surrounding area, much of which supported the King, whilst the town supported Parliament.

It became customary after the Reformation for wealthy residents to leave sums of money for almshouses for the poor, believing that charity was good for the soul. One such person was Matthew Chubb, who had been a bailiff of the town in about 1600: his fund is still being administered today.

In 1685 a most notorious series of trials took place following the rebellion led by the Duke of Monmouth. Many people from Dorset joined what has become known as the 'pitchfork army', and marched with Monmouth to Sedgemoor in Somerset where they were routed by the army of James II. The king was determined to show that he would not tolerate such uprisings, and sent Judge Jeffreys to conduct the assize. Of those tried in Dorchester, 74 men were hanged, drawn and quartered, 172 were transported to the Caribbean sugar plantations, and many more were whipped.

In the 18th century the town began to grow, and many of the merchants started building themselves better houses. Many of these are still standing, including Wollaston House in Charles Street. In the latter half of the century, the Assizes were held in the Antelope Hotel for a time; this was to allow the crumbling Guildhall in High West Street to be rebuilt. When it opened in 1797, the new building was called the Shire Hall. Many of the houses and shops we see today were built during the 18th century; they may have been altered at ground level, but if the visitor cares to look up they will see much that is architecturally pleasing.

In the 19th century the arrival of the railway allowed many people to travel further than before. Thomas Hardy, for instance, the great novelist and poet, was taken as a boy to London by his mother; it was a journey he remembered all his life. Many of Hardy's writings are set in Dorset and Dorchester, which he called Casterbridge.

In 1834 the infamous trial of the Tolpuddle martyrs took place. The unrest in the countryside from the 1820s had included the 'swing riots', the burning of haystacks and the destruction of the new agricultural machinery. A group of men from the village of Tolpuddle, who were trying to form a union in the hope of fair wages and an improvement in their living standards, were arrested and accused of taking a secret oath that was against the law. Found guilty by a jury which was mainly composed of landowners, their sentence was to be transported to Australia. Following the subsequent outcry in the press and from the populace, they were pardoned and returned to England.

The last public execution was held in 1856

when Martha Brown was hanged by the gate of Dorchester prison; the hanging was witnessed by the young Thomas Hardy.

The Eldridge Pope Brewery began life in the Green Dragon Inn in Durngate Street. In 1880 the brewery moved to new premises on the Weymouth Road, close to the railway, which took the beer to London.

Towards the end of the 19th century, a new estate was built to house the growing population. It was sited to the south of the town, and was called Victoria Park. In the 20th century a further development, to the west of the town at Poundbury, was also built.

In recent years, during building developments in the town, some of Dorchester's underlying history has been found. Archaeologists have discovered much of Durnovaria only inches below the surface. A Roman bath complex was found in 1977, and in the 1980s the huge postholes of another Neolithic henge were revealed. Their position has been marked in Waitrose's basement car park. In the summer of 2001, during the re-development of the old hospital site in Princes Street, another Roman mosaic was found. There is no doubt that much of the history of this fascinating town is still to be unearthed, and the most interesting archeological remains probably lie under the present buildings.

West

Bridport Road c1950 D44030
This view looks along the Via Iceniana, which linked London with
Exeter; it is very straight, as most Roman roads are. Nowadays,
beyond the ribbon development, the suburb of Poundbury has
blossomed. Under the guidance of the Prince of Wales, the
developers have produced an integrated mix of residential and
business property which has met with national acclaim.

◄ **The Dorset Regiment Museum c1955** D44073
The museum opened in 1955 and was refurbished in 1995. Among many exhibits is a desk from Hitler's Berlin Chancellery. The buildings on the left of the keep have been demolished. The Regent petrol station has been swept away to make more room for the Top o'Town car park.

The Dorset Regiment Museum c1955

D44063

This is the gateway built in 1879 to guard the earlier 19th-century barracks behind. This replaced the tented camp, which spread over Poundbury hillfort at the time of the threat of invasion by Napoleon. The old barrack buildings are now mostly used by the Royal Mail. The gateway (which has Queen Victoria's cipher above) has become the Keep Museum, celebrating the men of the old Dorset Regiment and the amalgamated Devon and Dorset Regiment which was formed in 1958.

High West Street c1965

D44096

This large roundabout is much smaller today. It stands where the great west gate of Durnovaria (Roman Dorchester) once stood. The two red telephone boxes on the right are still in use, and are still red. The buildings on the left date from the 17th, 18th and 19th centuries. It is a good idea to look up at them: the upper floors and roofs of these old buildings are much less changed, and more pleasing to the eye.

High West Street 1913

65615

Horse troughs were once a common sight. The one on the left was given to Dorchester in 1888 in memory of Major Vincent Wing RHA; it can now be found in the Fairfield car park. Beside it is a drinking fountain, which stands close to where the aqueduct entered the Roman town. Notice how elegant the ladies are in their late Edwardian costume.

High West Street 1891 28515
Although this is a busy shopping street, it contains some very pleasant houses. The second property on the left is Savernake House, which is built of local Broadmayne brick. High-wheeled perambulators are the only traffic, whilst pedestrians stand looking at the camera. Elegant gas lamps stand on either side of the road.

▼ **High West Street 1922** 72737

This view was taken thirty-one years after the previous photograph. The scene has hardly changed. There are many wrought iron railings and a balcony: these were typical of the Regency period, when such adornment of a house gave prestige to the owner.

▼ **High West Street c1950** D44031

Twenty-eight years later, the scene is now dominated by the increase in motor vehicles, and particularly by the bus bound for West Bay. The 'No Waiting' sign has arrived, but all the railings are gone. The street lighting is now electric and strung across the roadway.

▲ **High West Street 1930**
83390
On the right, the signwriting on the bow-fronted Post Office building is typical of advertising at this time, including the large 'roll films' on the extreme right. The Post Office is also a bookshop: diversity is always more profitable. A lady and a child stand outside, smartly-dressed in cloche hats.

High West Street c1960
D44081

It is thirty years after No 83390, and the signwriting on the Post Office has gone. The Old Teahouse is one of the few 17th-century buildings remaining in Dorchester. The Wessex restaurant and guesthouse, now the Wessex Royale Hotel, has a new sign. There are plaques for Goodyear tyres, Rootes cars and the Automobile Association. The road now has white centre markings, which seem to have come to Dorchester rather late.

**High West Street
1930** 83391
Outside the modern
building on the
right is a Crossley
car, which was
first registered
in March 1927.
There is a window
cleaner's handcart
on the left, and
someone appears
to be cleaning the
windows above J T
Godwin, the china
shop. Notice the
early coach on
the left; perhaps it
belongs to the King
Alfred School of
Winchester.

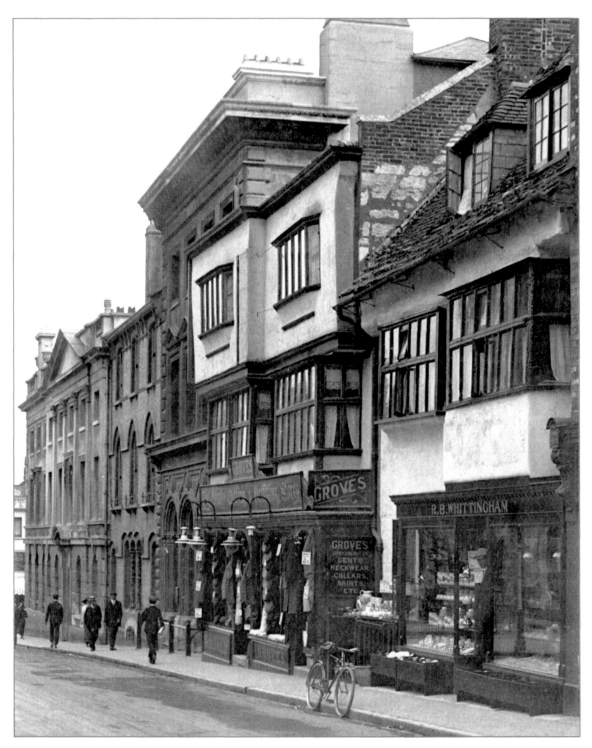

Judge Jeffreys' Lodgings 1913 65614A
Groves, a gentlemen's outfitters, occupy the 17th-century house in which the notorious judge lodged. He spent a few days in Dorchester during September 1685 following the Monmouth rebellion, when he presided over the savage 'bloody assizes'. The building later became an antique shop.

Judge Jeffreys' Lodgings 1930 83392

When we compare this view with No 65614A, we see that the premises have hardly altered; they have now become a restaurant, with a portrait of the 'hanging judge' suspended outside. Thurman's general hardware shop, on the left, was in business here for over 150 years. Next door is Handel House, which was a music shop.

A Singer Car 1930 83393V

This is a closer view of the car in the previous picture. This Singer Junior was first registered in Dorset in November 1929. The vehicle cost about £140, and had a top speed of 56 miles per hour. It has an AA badge on the grille, and the starting handle hangs over the number plate. The spare wheel is attached over the running board, while the battery sits on the nearside running board, out of the picture.

High West Street c1950 D44019
On the left, in front of St Peter's church, stands the statue of William Barnes (1801-1886), the Dorset dialect poet - the statue is a bronze by Roscoe Mullins. Barnes ran a local school and later became a church minister. His writings were well received in his time, and he later had a great influence on the young Thomas Hardy. On the left is the Dorset County Museum, built to the neo-Gothic design of Benjamin Ferrey in 1880. Thomas Hardy's study has been moved to the museum from Max Gate, Hardy's house.

High West Street c1950 D44022
This view is taken looking back up towards the Top o'Town. The ornate arched building on the left is the YMCA. In the distance, the Portland stone front of the Old Shire Hall, built in 1797, stands out with its distinctive flagpole on top; here, the old criminal court room is kept as a memorial to the Tolpuddle Martyrs.

The Roman Connection

Maiden Castle 1913 65617
For centuries, travellers along the road from Weymouth have
wondered at the huge Iron Age hill fort rising out of the
landscape, and many have been astonished to discover that it
is man-made. The earlier Neolithic long barrow and the Bronze
Age round barrows also to be seen here all show that ancient
peoples have used this area over a very long period.

▼ Maiden Castle Earthworks c1950 D44008
In the Iron Age, the Durotriges tribe developed this settlement and built huge defensive ditches. The tribe was overwhelmed by the Roman army in around 44AD. Around 70AD, the Durotriges were re-settled by the Romans in Durnovaria.

▼ The Amphitheatre 1891 28521
Maumbury Ring, as it is known today, was originally a Neolithic henge monument. It was adapted by the Romans for drilling troops, and later for entertaining the local populace with 'bread and circuses'. The railway station, which opened in 1847, is in the background. We can see the tall chimney of the Eldridge Pope brewery on the skyline.

▲ The Roman Amphitheat
1922 72756
The trees are hiding the encroaching suburbs. In th 17th century, during the C War, the Parliamentarians used the embankment as a strongpoint from which to defend the Weymouth Roa In the 18th century, this w a place for public executio including that of Mary Channing, who was strang and burnt here for the mur of her elderly husband. Th judiciary were benevolent enough to allow her to giv birth to her child before th executed her.

◄ **Roman Excavations
c1950** D44001
These are some of the
oldest walls in Dorchester.
This town house was built
by an affluent, high-status
Romano-British family. It
was discovered in the late
1930s, and it is a lasting
memorial to the importance
of the town the Romans
built. These are the only
remains of a Roman
town house to be seen in
England.

◄ The Nappers Mite c1960
D44077

We can see the stone mullion windows and low doorways of this former almshouse, which was built under the will of Robert Napier in 1616. The lower front has been altered, and the occupiers advertise their wares with metal signs. The old workhouse clock is supported by a decorative stone corbel and corbel bracket. The building beyond was the old Hardye's Grammar School, rebuilt in 1882. The Nappers Mite Coffee Lounge is still trading.

South Street

◄ **South Street c1950**
D44009
On the left, above the fourth sunblind, is a plaque informing the passer-by that Thomas Hardy was apprenticed here in 1856. On the adjoining wall is a plaque with the information that William Barnes lived here at about the same time - the older poet influenced the younger. The ladies carry wicker shopping baskets: there is not a plastic carrier bag in sight. The car in the foreground is a Vauxhall.

◄ **Thomas Hardye's School c1965** D44122
This is a modern replacement for the earlier building in South Street. The school was founded in 1579 by an earlier Thomas Hardye. The Grammar School was moved to this site in the late 1920s: Thomas Hardy laid the foundation stone in October 1927, and it was opened in May 1928 by the then Prince of Wales. The school is now a comprehensive.

The Post Office 1913 65612
This is a grand, imposing building, erected in the early 20th
century in the Georgian style at a time when the British Empire
was at the height of its power and influence; it is unchanged in
appearance today. The red brick contrasts with the white Portland
stone quoins. The mullions of the bow window are Ionic pillars, and
so are the broken pilasters supporting the arched doorway.

South Street c1950 D44037
Goulds have been in the town for over 50 years, and are still trading. Stroud's confectionery advertises itself with prominent signwriting, which was popular at the time. All three buildings on the right are of distinctive Broadmayne brick. Further on, the buildings were demolished during the 1980s, including the Wesleyan Chapel. It is clear that dress codes have relaxed; we can see at least two men without ties.

South Street c1965 D44123
More national chain stores have moved into the town by now; they include K shoes, and Timothy Whites where Boons once traded. The greengrocer still sellls from his barrow in almost the same spot today. We can see an interesting selection of cars, including a Hillman Minx, a Vauxhall Estate and a Ford Cortina on the right.

Cornhill

Cornhill 1891 28514
The Antelope Hotel was one of Dorchester's important coaching inns. Built of brick with stylish bow windows on two floors, it has a decorative wrought iron balcony and an ornate lamp. Note the stone wheel guards at ground level to protect the walls from the wheels of the carriages entering the arch. Towards the end of the 18th century, the Antelope was used for court hearings while the Shire Hall was rebuilt. The round sign above the awning advertises Mortimers Boot Store. We can see the chancel of St Peter's church on the opposite side of the junction with High West Street, and on the right the Town Hall stands at the head of High East Street.

Cornhill 1903 50841
The decorative globe
lamps on the right
are new at this date.
Shop goods spill out
on to the pavement:
the policeman (centre)
would have been a
regular sight, and
therefore a deterrent
to shoplifting. On the
corner of the street
the bow windows have
been replaced by an
18th-century style
Lloyds Bank. Fresh
bread is being delivered
by handcart.

Cornhill 1922 72741
The Antelope now has its name boldly painted across the upper
storey. Robinson's shop has become the City and Midland Bank.
The Antelope now welcomes motor carriages, rather than the
horse-drawn coaches for which it was built.

Cornhill 1930 83389
Looking south, we can see the tall chimney of the brewery and
the spire of the Congregational Chapel standing together on the
skyline. The bus now brings people into the town for shopping, as
the larger chains such as Boots and Freeman Hardy & Willis begin
to appear. The family name of Pouncy has been prominent in the
business and governance of Dorchester since the 17th century.
The tap for the pump is still in place on the monument.

Cornhill c1950 D44020
This is probably where the
Roman forum, or market
place, developed. Dorchester
market continued here well
into the 20th century, when it
moved to its present position
beside the Weymouth Road.
Pouncy's shop has become
Parsons, and the Antelope
Hotel now has an RAC sign.
The Belisha beacon indicates
a pedestrian crossing, which
is marked only by studs at this
date.
The car passing the cupola
monument is a Ford 8.

Cornhill c1950 D44036
The 'No Waiting' sign outside Boons general store shows that parking on this side of the street is only on even-numbered days. The street market is busy. The front car is an Austin, which was first registered to a man from Milborne Port in February 1934. The rear of this motor car appears in picture number D44028 (page 45).

Cornhill c1965 D44111
Judging by the Town Hall clock, it must be closing time for offices and shops. The Post Box no longer stands at the junction. Freeman Hardy Willis, a well-known shoe chain, still stands on the right.

Cornhill c1965 D44113
This view looks south down the Cornhill. On the wall, alongside the open delivery van, is a plaque in memory of Sir Frederick Treves, who was born in 1850. He was a renowned surgeon, and is probably best remembered for rescuing the unfortunate John Merrick, who was known as the Elephant Man.

The Old Pump and the Town Hall 1913 65611
This monument, which was built on the site of the old market cupola in 1784, was also the town pump. A pillar box in the middle of the carriageway, shows how little the traffic impeded the pedestrians in posting their letters.

The Old Pump and the Town Hall 1913 65610
The Town Hall was built in 1848, and the clock tower was added in 1861. The townsfolk named the tower 'Galpins Folly', because they did not believe that the slender column would support its weight - but it is still standing. The monument now has a gas lamp attached to it.

The Churches

High West Street c1950 D44028
Holy Trinity Church was mentioned in the Domesday Book of
1088; inside there is a list of serving clergy since 1302. The
present building is the fifth on the site, and was designed by
Benjamin Ferrey in 1876. The church is unique in that it was
transferred from the Church of England to the Roman Catholic
community in 1976. We can see the rear of the Austin car, JT
479, which we saw in picture No 44036 (page 43)

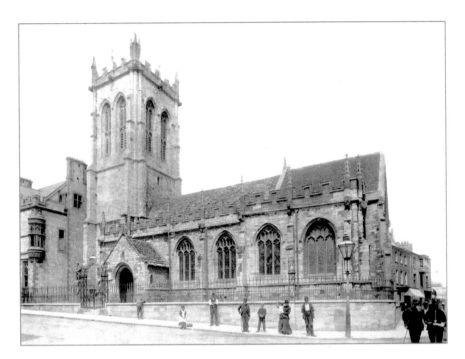

St Peter's Church 1891 28520
This is now the parish church of Dorchester. It features a 15th-century Perpendicular tower, and a 12th-century front porch, beneath which lie the remains of John White, who was the former rector of both Holy Trinity and St Peter's. There are three different types of stone used in this building: the golden Ham Hill stone, a blue lias and Purbeck marble.

St Peter's Church 1922 72749
In this later view, we can see the memorial cross to the parish members who died in World War I in front of the second window from the right. The site of the former shambles, or meat market, is visible between the buildings. Also visible is the gateway to the prison, which features in Thomas Hardy's 'Far from the Madding Crowd'.

High East Street 1891 28513
This is All Saints Church, the church of the third and smallest parish in Dorchester. The original medieval church was burnt in the great fire of 1613, and it was again rebuilt by Benjamin Ferrey in 1876. The spire beautifully enhances the High Street skyline, but the building is now closed and redundant. It is used by the Museum as a store for the many as yet unexhibited artefacts.

St Mary's Church, Victoria Park c1965 D44093
This church, built in the Gothic style, was erected in the early 20th-century to serve the spreading Victorian suburbs of Dorchester. It is now frequently used for musical events, especially at Christmas time.

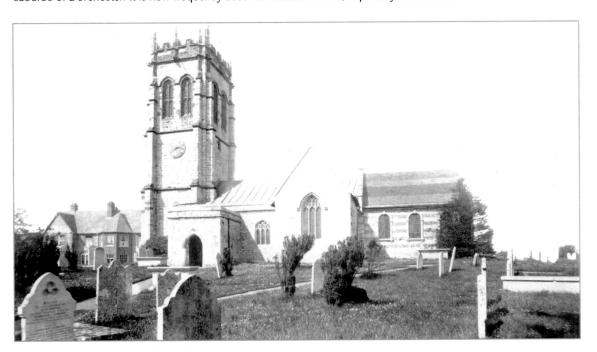

Fordington, St George's Church 1898 41164
The church stands proudly above the village, which used to be totally separated from Dorchester. The much-restored church was first built in the Middle Ages, and the Perpendicular tower is 15th-century. In 1840 the bones of an Iron Age horse, together with its bridle, were discovered beneath the chancel.

East

High East Street c1950 D44034
This view looks east; the roadway is narrower here. The trees on
the horizon are in Kingston Maurward park. The street looks a
more busy and prosperous part of the town than it is today. On
the left, two men take their ease in the deep-set windows of the
Cornmarket Hall.

**The King's Arms
Hotel 1913** 65626
This started as a
coaching inn about
three hundred years
ago; the hotel has
since been altered and
rebuilt. Thomas Hardy
was a regular customer,
and he used it in several
of his novels. An early
AA sign
hangs above the floral
decoration. Both horse-
drawn and horseless
carriages demonstrate
the changes in
transport.

High East Street 1891 28512
From when he was eight years old, Thomas Hardy walked along these pavements into town, firstly to go to school, and secondly to go to work at the office of Crickmay, the architect, to whom he was apprenticed. This scene would have been very familiar to him. These close-packed houses, mostly dating from the 18th century, are not as large, or as grand, as those higher up the street.

High East Street 1913 65613
On the left is Channons the motor engineers; this was possibly the
first garage in the town. Note the pediment over the adjoining front
door, where business and residential accommodation is still very
cheek by jowl. Wood's general stores encroach onto the pavement.

High East Street 1922 72739

There is a notice about electric driving lamps in the engineer's window on the left, a reminder that many vehicles were still equipped only with the oil variety at this date. The building on the right behind the railings is now the Casterbridge Hotel; it stands on the site of the former gaol that was replaced at the end of the 18th century.

High East Street c1950 D44013

In the foreground is a military vehicle, possibly from the barracks. A large hoarding advertising Fry's Chocolate on the side of the building replaces the signwriting. On the left is a pub sign for the Borough Arms, which appears in several of Hardy's novels, including 'Under the Greenwood Tree'. Further down on the right was the Phoenix, the scene of Hardy's poem 'The Dance at the Phoenix'.

The Grove 1922 72755
This road is the A357
to Yeovil and Bristol.
The cottages are
outside the line of the
old walls, and may not
have been subjected to
the ban on thatch which
followed the fires of the
17th century. The trees
are those of the adjacent
Colliton Walk.

The Walks

◄ **Colliton Walk 1898**
41155
The walks, which surround the town along the line of the Roman walls, were laid out during the 18th century. By the time of this photograph, the trees, planted with such foresight, have begun to mature. The pillars mark the entrance to Colliton Park, now home to the Art Deco offices of the Dorset County Council and the Magistrates Court.

◄ **South Walks 1898**
41153
The trees along South Walks are all horse chestnuts, a delight in late spring when their 'candles' are in full bloom. On the right are some of the large houses which were built outside the line of the old town walls after the railway arrived. On the left, an impressive hexagonal post box, with VRI neatly inscribed on it, dates from about 1860.

▼ The Cenotaph 1922 72752
The memorial, built of Portland stone, was dedicated in 1921, and is inscribed with 237 names. Carved above the long list of names is a laurel wreath, the reward for heroes, which surrounds a cross. The walls outside the houses on the right, and the post box and the trees, appear not to have changed - and yet the world has changed radically since the First World War.

▼ West Walks 1903 50843
The walk follows the line of original Roman ditches. Three ditches, together with a wall, were constructed as defences around the town; they took about 50 years to complete.

▲ West Walks 1922 72746
Behind the fencing on the right is the site of the former Dorset County Hospital, which has recently been re-located to the west of the town. In 2001, during redevelopment, a number of Roman finds were made, including the remains of a mosaic-floored room; this was part of another high-status house of the Roman period.

The Borough Gardens
1898 41158a

The gardens were laid out by the corporation in 1896 for the residents to enjoy at their leisure. The bushes and trees are all mostly immature at this date. The houses behind are in Cornwall Road, and are sitting on the outer Roman ditch. This ditch is over 100 yards from the line of the Roman wall, and gives some clue to the immensity of the fortifications.

The Borough Gardens 1922 72751
The trees and bushes are now maturing. An addition to the gardens is the clock, which was presented by Charles Hansford in 1905. It was made in the Lott and Walne foundry of Fordington, which closed in 1932. We can also see the well-maintained tennis courts on the left.

The Borough Gardens 1922 72750
The bandstand, donated to the town by Colonel WE Brymer MP, opened on 28 July 1898; it gives pleasure to many people to this day, when the town band entertains. The gardens are used by many people in the summer for a picnic lunch away from the office. In more recent years, a children's playground has been introduced.

The River

The View from the River Frome 1930 83388
The water meadows are on the north side of the town, and from
them we can see the tower of St Peter's and the spire of All Saints'
rising proudly above the crowded roofs.

Farm Cottages 1894
34531
These cottages were
at Coker's Frome farm;
they fell into decay in
the early 20th century.
They attracted many
artists, and a number of
paintings and engravings
are still in existence.
The cottages are typical
of agricultural workers'
homes of the time,
with small rooms and
windows; the interiors
were very dark, and lit
only by oil lamps. To the
right were other farm
buildings and the more
substantial slate-roofed
farmhouse, which burned
down; the present
farmhouse was built in the
mid 20th century. The
river runs on the left, and
formed a lake. The Mayo
family, who have owned
and farmed the land since
1848, still do so today.

▼ **The View from the River 1894** 34530
We can see the high chimneys of the prison on the right. It was first built on the site of the old castle in 1792, but the present building has been adapted by the Victorians. In the foreground is the River Frome, and the remains of a hatch which would have controlled the flow into the dyke.

▼ **A Bridge on the Frome 1913** 65621
This river pathway is close to the centre of the town; a substantial little footbridge adjoins a ford in the river. The scene has the appearance of a drove for cattle leaving the winter fields near the town to feed in the water meadows.

▲ **Blue Bridge
the River Frome 1922**
72753
This bridge is still very close to the town centre; it crosses the Frome carrying a pathway which is used by many today as a relaxing walk. A boy is paddling in the shallows, and on the right his companion appears to be fishing.

◄ **The River Frome 1930**
83396
This tranquil scene shows
the river skirting around the
east of the town. Perhaps
this is a kissing gate; the
scene is certainly romantic,
with the trees leaning down
low as they do in William
Barnes' poem 'Linden Lea'.

▼ **The View from the Frome Bridge 1913** 65619
A mixed herd of cattle are grazing on the grass of the meadows, which are always lush because of the water close by. Among the trees on the left, one man appears to be repairing the fence, watched by another. The church in the far background is in Fordington.

▼ **The View from the Fields 1891** 28509
We are looking west, towards Fordington. The river banks are reinforced by wooden planks, which form part of the sluices, or hatches, which allow the meadows to be flooded in the spring. In the background, St George's Church stands high above the village roofs which crowd in on all sides.

▲ **The Water Meadows 1891** 28510
This view was taken from further along the river. It is a scene that Thomas Hardy would have seen every day on his way to school, and he later used it in 'The Mayor of Casterbridge'. We can see the water meadows if we travel along the Dorchester bypass.

◄ **Grey's Bridge 1894** 34537
This bridge is named after
Mrs Laura Pitt, neé Grey.
She had the bridge built in
the 18th century because
she was tired of her carriage
wheels breaking in the
ford. In this photograph,
children are standing where,
according to Thomas Hardy,
the shameful people of the
town used to gather.

Kingston Park 1903 50842
A swan glides gently by as the river continues on its way to
Wareham, and on to the sea at Poole Harbour. The River Frome
passes through the park of Kingston Maurward House, which is
about a mile east of the town. The house was built in the 18th
century in the classical style a few hundred yards away from the
Tudor manor, which is still standing. It is said that when George III
visited, he remarked to the owner: 'Brick, Mr Pitt?' When the king
next visited, the bricks had been encased with Portland stone. The
house is now a centre for further education in farming and country
pursuits. The gardens are open to the public.

Around Dorchester

The Hangman's Cottage 1894 34535
This cottage is so named because legend has it that when Judge
Jeffreys came to town, the hangman accompanying him stayed
here. An elderly man who visited the cottage in the 1920s as
a child tells that there were no stairs, but a rope ladder
through a trap door to the upper floor, which was for the
hangman's safety.

**By the Millstream
1913** 65618X
A young couple, dressed
in their best clothes,
pose beside the sluices
on the millstream; the
railing on the left is
around the old millpond,
but the mill has long
gone. The Hangman's
Cottage is in the
background.

The Hangman's Cottage 1898 41163

There is little difference in the four years between this and photograph No 34535. Two children play safely on the roadside. The large house in the background has since been demolished, and several new homes have been built on the site. The trees today are fully-grown, and hide and shade the area.

Puddletown, The Post Office and High Street c1955

P163066

The village, whose name dervies from the River Piddle which flows close by, straddles the once busy A35. There are many thatched cottages of various dates here, some with leaded light windows. Thomas Hardy's grandfather was born in the village, and it features in 'Far from the Madding Crowd' as Weatherbury. Close by is the 15th-century Athelhampton House, which stands in lovely gardens.

Puddletown High Street c1955

P163028

A new bypass has recently been completed and local trade has suffered, including the closure of the Prince of Wales Inn. Along the street on the right, the former butcher's shop was once owned by Ralph Wightman, a well-known author and broadcaster; he regularly appeared on the BBC programme 'Any Questions?' His family farmed in the Piddle valley.

Puddletown, The Square c1955 P163011
The attractive thatched house with the bow window supported by pillars dominates the centre of the village. The road on the right leads to the church, dedicated to St Mary and built between the 12th and the 15th centuries. The interior contains much Jacobean furniture, including a three-tier pulpit with a high tester. The Lord's Prayer is painted on the north wall. There are some interesting effigies, including one of a former crusader. Another effigy portrays a knight who probably fought in the Wars of the Roses, for the links of the chain attached to his armour are joined by the roses of York. Puddletown features in many of Thomas Hardy's novels as Weatherbury.

Tolpuddle Pixies' Cottage c1955 T154009
This is typical of the style of a Dorset village house, with low thatched roof and thatched porches. The sign on the wall offers coffees, accommodation, teas and lunches.

Tolpuddle The Martyrs' Tree and Seat c1955 T154029
This thatched shelter, with the commemorative seats, marks the spot where the alleged meeting took place between the six men, led by George Loveless, who became known as the Tolpuddle Martyrs. The seat was presented in 1934 by Sir Ernest Debenham to mark the centenary of their trial and transportation to Australia.

◀ **West Stafford
St Andrew's Church
c1955** W628076
The church is over
six hundred years old,
and was first altered in
1640. There is still
much remaining of
the Jacobean period,
including the royal arms
of James I. The church
is said to be the one in
which Hardy's Tess of
the D'Urbervilles was
wed to Angel Clare.

Osmington, The Post Office Stores c1955 074042
A little further down the hill that we see in No O74048 is the post office; it has now closed, but the same thatched cottages remain. The surrounding area, close to the sea, was a centre for smuggling during the 18th century. Especially remembered as a smuggler is Pierre Latour, or French Pete, as he was known.

▼ **West Stafford, Thatching c1960** W628082
The art of thatching is still much in demand throughout Dorset. Local thatch was originally made of wheat, rye or barley straw, but now longer-lasting reed is often used. The purpose of the covers on the chimneys is to prevent sparks igniting the roof.

◄ **Osmington, Lychgate Cottage c1955** 074048
This is a very attractive village, with a narrow street and thatched cottages. The lychgate stands at the entrance to the churchyard. The church is dedicated to St Osmund and has a 15th-century tower, although most of the fabric is from about 1840. The English landscape painter John Constable painted 'Weymouth Bay' here while he was on his honeymoon.

Upwey, The Wishing Well 1894 34554a
The tea gardens here are still delightful. The spring is the headwater of the River Wey, which flows only four miles to the sea. There were said to be medicinal advantages in the water, and King George III visited during his summers in Weymouth from 1789-1805. The cup he used is said to be the Gold Cup, the most prestigious prize at Royal Ascot.

**Upwey
St Lawrence's Church
and the Village c1870**
8058
Standing above the
houses on a small
knoll, the church of
St Lawrence has been
here since Saxon times.
Little remains of the
early building; most of
the fabric dates from
the 14th and 15th
centuries. Inside, the
church is unusual in
that York roses are
painted on the walls.
A stone carving of the
green man of Celtic
legend stands on top
of a column; the green
man appears in many
Dorset churches,
where old habits and
beliefs die hard. The
picturesque thatched
cottages close to the
church remain, but the
village is now much
larger - 20th-century
development and many
more trees cover the
hillside.

◄ **Abbotsbury
The Swannery c1955**
A2039
The swannery was probably
created to provide food for
the abbey on high days.
The monks made a duck
decoy tunnel to ensure that
the abbot's table was well
supplied. The Fleet, a strip
of brackish water between
the Chesil Beach and the
shoreline, gives a safe
haven to all kinds of wetland
fowl, including at one time a
stray flamingo.

Abbotsbury, Market Street c1955 A2027
The mostly 15th-century church of St Nicholas rises above the narrow street of stone cottages. Inside the church is a Jacobean pulpit, which is pierced by two bullet holes, remnants of the Civil War. The metal sign, partially obscured, is for Bev, a liquid coffee popular in World War II.

Abbotsbury The Barn 1890 27323
Here we see the back of the great tithe barn, which was built in about 1413. It was claimed to be one of the largest in the country at 276ft long. It is a reminder of the power of the church during the Middle Ages.

Frampton, The Bridge 1906 54586
The village takes its name from a corruption of the words 'Frome Town'. This graceful arched bridge over the River Frome has wooden rails, which still guard the road. The river is wide and prone to flooding, which does not deter the large duck family nesting under the bridge.

◄ **Charminster
East Hill c1955** C65025
Charminster was
mentioned in the
Domesday Book; it
was then known as
Cerminstre. The road
over the River Cerne
leads to a group of small,
neat cottages.
The village is the lowest
in the valley of the
Cerne, which meanders
around Dorchester
before joining the
Frome.

◄ **Frampton**
The Village 1906 54583
This row of flint and brick cottages are in the style of the 17th century, but they have the date 1844 over the porch. The windows are diamond-paned leaded lights with stone mullions and a dripstone over the upper window. Where the wall stood on the right, the now open space is an attractive riverside garden beside the village hall.

▼ **Charminster, The Church and the War Memorial 1922** 72759
The river runs alongside the right of the churchyard. The church building includes parts of an 11th-century pre-Norman church, with further additions being spread over the next eight hundred years. In the background is the war memorial and several thatched cottages . The church of St Mary was recently damaged by flooding.

◄ **Charminster**
The Bridge 1922
72760X
This footbridge is still to be found in the village. The young man may be delivering post, judging by his bag. He is apparently travelling on two wheels, as he is wearing bicycle clips. His straw boater is in the fashion of the time.

Thomas Hardy

Stinsford
Thomas Hardy's Cottage c1955 S771071
The poet and novelist was born in this cottage on
3 June 1840. It was built by his grandfather, and
Thomas Hardy lived here with his parents and one
brother and two sisters. The National Trust now
owns the cottage.

Thomas Hardy's Home 1930 83401
Max Gate was Hardy's home for fifty-three years. He designed
the house, and his brother Henry built it in 1885. The sundial
on the wall was erected after his death, but it was his design; it is
inscribed 'Quid de nocte', which translates as 'what of night?'. In the
garden are the graves of his pets, including that of his dog Wessex.

Thomas Hardy's Home 1930 83402
Hardy lived here at Max Gate with his first wife Emma Gifford, who died in 1912. In 1914, he married Florence Dugdale, and they entertained many of the literary names of the day, including T E Lawrence and J M Barrie. Hardy died in this house on 11 January 1928. This house is also now in the care of the National Trust.

Stinsford, St Michael's Church 1930 83397
This is a place of pilgrimage for admirers of Hardy. The church and graveyard have been immortalised in his poems and novels. The church is small, and dates from Norman times, with many later additions. In recent years the choir gallery has been replaced; there is a memorial to Hardy's grandfather, father and uncle, who played in the choir band in the original gallery. The band was the inspiration for his novel 'Under the Greenwood Tree'.

▲ **Stinsford, The Churchyard**
Thomas Hardy's Grave 1930 83398
The heart of Thomas Hardy lies in this grave,
together with both his wives. His body was
cremated, and the ashes were interred in
Westminster Abbey. The grave lies alongside
those of his sisters, his brother, his parents and
his grandparents. Further along the path is the
grave of Cecil Day Lewis, 1904-1972, the
Poet Laureate, buried close to his literary
mentor.

The Thomas Hardy Memorial c1965 D44101 ▶
Close to the Top o'Town, Dorset's most famous
son is commemorated in this life-size bronze
statue by Eric Kennington, set on a Portland
stone plinth. Unveiled by Sir James Barrie in
1931, the statue shows Hardy seated and
dressed for the country, wearing a jacket and
leather gaiters, with his hat on his knee. Around
the figure are plants and animals, symbolizing
Hardy's love for his native countryside.

Index

FRITH PRODUCTS & SERVICES

Francis Frith would doubtless be pleased to know that the pioneering publishing venture he started in 1860 still continues today. Over a hundred and forty years later, The Francis Frith Collection continues in the same innovative tradition and is now one of the foremost publishers of vintage photographs in the world. Some of the current activities include:

INTERIOR DECORATION

Today Frith's photographs can be seen framed and as giant wall murals in thousands of pubs, restaurants, hotels, banks, retail stores and other public buildings throughout the country. In every case they enhance the unique local atmosphere of the places they depict and provide reminders of gentler days in an increasingly busy and frenetic world.

PRODUCT PROMOTIONS

Frith products are used by many major companies to promote the sales of their own products or to reinforce their own history and heritage. Frith promotions have been used by Hovis bread, Courage beers, Scots Porage Oats, Colman's mustard, Cadbury's foods, Mellow Birds coffee, Dunhill pipe tobacco, Guinness, and Bulmer's Cider.

GENEALOGY AND FAMILY HISTORY

As the interest in family history and roots grows world-wide, more and more people are turning to Frith's photographs of Great Britain for images of the towns, villages and streets where their ancestors lived; and, of course, photographs of the churches and chapels where their ancestors were christened, married and buried are an essential part of every genealogy tree and family album.

FRITH PRODUCTS

All Frith photographs are available Framed or just as Mounted Prints and Posters (size 23 x 16 inches). These may be ordered from the address below. Other products available are - Address Books, Calendars, Jigsaws, Canvas Prints, Postcards and local and prestige books.

THE INTERNET

Already ninety thousand Frith photographs can be viewed and purchased on the internet through the Frith websites and a myriad of partner sites.

For more detailed information on Frith products, look at this site:
www.francisfrith.com

See the complete list of Frith Books at: www.francisfrith.com
This web site is regularly updated with the latest list of publications from The Francis Frith Collection. If you wish to buy books relating to another part of the country that your local bookshop does not stock, you may purchase on-line.

For further information, trade, or author enquiries please contact us at the address below:
The Francis Frith Collection, Unit 6, Oakley Business Park, Wylye Road, Dinton, Wiltshire SP3 5EU.
Tel: +44 (0)1722 716 376 Fax: +44 (0)1722 716 881   Email: sales@francisfrith.co.uk

See Frith products on the internet at www.francisfrith.com

FREE PRINT OF YOUR CHOICE
CHOOSE A PHOTOGRAPH FROM THIS BOOK
+ £3.80 POSTAGE

Mounted Print
Overall size 14 x 11 inches (355 x 280mm)

TO RECEIVE YOUR FREE PRINT

Choose any Frith photograph in this book
Simply complete the Voucher opposite and return it with your remittance for £3.50 (to cover postage and handling) and we will print the photograph of your choice in SEPIA (size 11 x 8 inches) and supply it in a cream mount ready to frame (overall size 14 x 11 inches).

Order additional Mounted Prints
at HALF PRICE - £12.00 each (normally £24.00)
If you would like to order more Frith prints from this book, possibly as gifts for friends and family, you can buy them at half price (with no additional postage costs).

Have your Mounted Prints framed
For an extra £20.00 per print you can have your mounted print(s) framed in an elegant polished wood and gilt moulding, overall size 16 x 13 inches (no additional postage required).

IMPORTANT!

❶ Please note: aerial photographs and photographs with a reference number starting with a "Z" are not Frith photographs and cannot be supplied under this offer.

❷ Offer valid for delivery to one UK address only.

❸ These special prices are only available if you use this form to order. You must use the ORIGINAL VOUCHER on this page (no copies permitted). We can only despatch to one UK address.

❹ This offer cannot be combined with any other offer.

As a customer your name & address will be stored by Frith but not sold or rented to third parties. Your data will be used for the purpose of this promotion only.

Send completed Voucher form to:
The Francis Frith Collection,
19 Kingsmead Business Park, Gillingham,
Dorset SP8 5FB

Voucher for *FREE* and Reduced Price *Frith Prints*

Please do not photocopy this voucher. Only the original is valid, so please fill it in, cut it out and return it to us with your order.

Picture ref no	Page no	Qty	Mounted @ £12.00	Framed + £20.00	Total Cost £
		1	Free of charge*	£	£
			£12.00	£	£
			£12.00	£	£
			£12.00	£	£
			£12.00	£	£
			£12.00	£	£

Please allow 28 days for delivery. Offer available to one UK address only.

* Post & handling		£3.80
Total Order Cost		£

Title of this book . . . .

I enclose a cheque/postal order for £ . . . .

made payable to 'The Francis Frith Collection'

OR please debit my Mastercard / Visa / Maestro card, details below

Card Number:

Issue No (Maestro only):   Valid from (Maestro):

Card Security Number: Expires:

Signature:

Name Mr/Mrs/Ms . . . .

Address . . . .

. . . .

. . . .

. . . . Postcode . . . .

Daytime Tel No . . . .

Email . . . .

Valid to 31/12/18

Can you help us with information about any of the Frith photographs in this book?

We are gradually compiling an historical record for each of the photographs in the Frith archive. It is always fascinating to find out the names of the people shown in the pictures, as well as insights into the shops, buildings and other features depicted.

If you recognize anyone in the photographs in this book, or if you have information not already included in the author's caption, do let us know. We would love to hear from you, and will try to publish it in future books or articles.

An Invitation from The Francis Frith Collection to Share Your Memories

The 'Share Your Memories' feature of our website allows members of the public to add personal memories relating to the places featured in our photographs, or comment on others already added. Seeing a place from your past can rekindle forgotten or long held memories. Why not visit the website, find photographs of places you know well and add YOUR story for others to read and enjoy? We would love to hear from you!

www.francisfrith.com/memories

Our production team

Frith books are produced by a small dedicated team at offices near Salisbury. Most have worked with the Frith Collection for many years. All have in common one quality: they have a passion for the Frith Collection.

Frith Books and Gifts

We have a wide range of books and gifts available on our website utilising our photographic archive, many of which can be individually personalised.

www.francisfrith.com